THE INCARNATION

Twenty-five Poems

For Advent

On the Word Made Flesh

Thomas Ryder Worth

Audio version of this publication is also available on iTunes, Amazon, & Audible.

Book design by www.greatwriting.org
www.incarnationpoems.org

Mother and Child; from a pencil sketch by Marsha Worth

A Note about the Poet and His Work

Tom Worth has been a pastor and Bible teacher in Pentecostal/Charismatic circles since the early eighties. For over twenty-five years he has made annual mission trips to Bulgaria where he teaches in the P/C churches there. He and his wife, Marsha, have been married for forty-four years. They have two daughters who are married and who have supplied them with five precious grandchildren. He holds the M. Div. and the D. Min. from Northeastern Seminary in Rochester, NY. He is currently the pastor of Community Covenant Church in Manlius, NY. He has served on the adjunct faculty of Pinecrest/Bethany and Northeastern Seminary. Tom has a poetic-narrative way of teaching and preaching from the Scriptures where he seeks to help people see Jesus in fresh ways.

Preface

I have been a pastor for over thirty years and a Bible teacher for almost forty. I have done mission work for over thirty years as well. But I have been a poet of the Incarnation the longest—forty-four years. For as long as Marsha and I have been married, I have written a Christmas poem almost every year. At other times of the year I have also pondered the Incarnation poetically. At Christmastime we would send a poem to our friends and family. The Mother & Child on the front is from a sketch Marsha prepared for a Christmas card we designed over forty years ago. This first collection comes as close as anything I have ever written to representing the heart and soul of what is meaningful to me.

Out of those forty-some odd poems I've written, I have selected twenty-five for this collection. You may think of it as a poetic Advent Calendar, with a poem for each day in December leading up to Christmas. That's about the right pace to take these in. Some will be quite short; others will be longer; but all will require some time for meditation.

May the Lord bless you as you make your way through my reflections on the Coming of our Lord Jesus.

T. R. W., Syracuse, New York

A Note about the Artist and Her Work

Tom Worth got to know Petrana Petsova over the course of his many mission trips to Silistra, Bulgaria. Petrana graduated from the School of Fine Arts in Sofia in 1979, while the country was deep in the grip of Communism. Even though she was forbidden to paint Christian or biblical subjects, she persevered and endured harassment and persecution. The authorities confiscated and destroyed her paintings. She came upon a novel way to hide them from the police. Because she kept bees in her back garden, she was able to hide her Christian paintings in her beehives. She could slide a frame of honeycomb out and slide a painting into the same slot. The bees kept watch over her work and she did not lose any more after that. Her home has become a picture gallery where her paintings line the walls and even the ceiling. She is quite elderly but vigorous, and she still paints for the glory of God and the love of the subject.

Table of Contents

Acknowledgments

I thank my wife Marsha, my most ardent encourager and truest critic. For any poem to see the light of day, it had to pass her muster first. I thank my daughters who always looked forward to what I would write for Christmas. I thank family, friends and folks at church who have been the recipients of these poems for the last four decades or more. I thank those who have fussed at me over the years, exhorting me to publish these reflections. I thank Jim Palumbo for seeking me out and showing me how it could be done. I thank World Challenge for providing the means to get me going. I thank Petrana Petsova for letting us publish some of her paintings to illustrate this collection, and Niki Markov for facilitating her contribution. And thank you, Jim Holmes, for putting it all together. Many thanks to all!

Foreword

I have known Thomas Ryder Worth for more than thirty years now and I consider him a dear friend, in some ways one of my best friends, but strangely not a close friend. As a matter of fact, we have probably spent no more than twenty or thirty days together in those decades. So, saying he is a best friend is probably a misstatement; he is a better kind of friend. By that, I mean that I enjoy the cadence of our fellowship. Spending time with Tom is like hearing that old chorus they used to sing when you first got saved—a song that was simple and right, unashamedly about Jesus and out of fashion today. Then again, maybe it is simply because we have a friend in common.

It makes me think of the story in John 21; a campfire on the beach, and Jesus calling out to Peter, James, John, Nathanael, and Thomas in their boat, two of whom had been fairweather friends only a few days earlier. "Friends," he calls out, "have you caught anything?" And after the great draught of fish, they see a campfire, and breakfast, and Jesus. For fishermen, a campfire is a sacred place for friends and fellowship.

Occasionally I imagine myself in various scenes in the Bible. Of all the scenes, I think I would feel most myself in this one—just the guys, after fishing, around a campfire with Jesus.

There are few people I know with whom that fire burns as bright. With Tom you are free from the usual self-interest, hidden agendas, and small-talk of pastors and preachers that drives one to boredom or to want to crawl out of your skin. There is no religious jargon or discussions of church-growth strategies or fund raising. There is just this friendship with Jesus; it is his most apparent attribute.

In the age of denominations, Pentecostals, Charismatics, and Evangelicals, Tom is still just Jesus People. This little book is not intended to be just beautiful, elegant, or whimsical, although it is, at times, that. Rather it is an expression given to us in such a deeply personal way, like one friend to another, of the author's heart in his two favorite things—friendship and Jesus.

The Incarnation is an extraordinary collection of writings that draws us closer to Jesus, that helps us know and love him in an unusually personal and intimate way. We are drawing him into our hearts at his most vulnerable, and perhaps most human time—at his Incarnation.

Jim Palumbo

The Angels Proclaim to the Shepherds the Good News about the Birth of the Savior.

An Advent Meditation

Our dog can sense a visitor a long way off.
He begins to growl and mutter in low tones.
During this Advent season I wait and look and long.
Do I sense a rumble in the distance?
I suppose I growl and mutter in my own way…

He, for whom the poets sang,
He, to whom the psalmists prayed,
He, about whom the wise pondered,
He, for whom the Exiles longed—
Draws near with a weight of glory.
He, for whom and by whom all things were made—is coming!

I sense the coming of him who defies description
Whose coming is so weighty it almost makes the earth tremble.
Creation seems to utter a subliminal groan,
Longing for all the prophets foretold.

Will heaven and earth lose their moorings
And flee away when he comes?
Or will the trees of the field clap their hands?
I get a sense in Advent of an approaching Immensity,
Something so huge and hard to comprehend—
And then, I hear the soft cries of a baby in a manger…

The Ways to Bethlehem

The Fullness of Time

"But when the fullness of the time was come,
God sent forth his Son, made of a woman…"
Galatians 4:4, KJV

Now Mary and Joseph make this long journey and at the end of it
no one is ready for them.
They themselves are not ready for his birth.
Mary's labor pains are probably induced
by the long ride on the back of a donkey,
the jolting and swaying, the up and down,
and now at the end of it,
Mary tells Joseph that her time is at hand…
the fullness of time.

He looks anxiously from house to house,
this place and that,
even the caravanserai, the inn, is too crowded
and there is no room for them.
The little town of Bethlehem is overcrowded by tired visitors,
come for the census,
feeling jerked around by the Romans,
feeling the nuisance, the upheaval,
and no one has time
for this weary couple in the fullness of time.

They find (or maybe someone finds for them) a stable,
perhaps a cave where farm animals are kept.
There in the night, on a pile of straw,
wishing for better,
but having to make do with what they have,
Mary gives way to the contractions
that will not be delayed or postponed—

the Child will come now and that is all there is to it—
in the fullness of time.

Mary gives birth in the cold night, in the stable,
perhaps no longer caring about the squalid surroundings,
caring only to get it over with.
And Joseph is the anxious and inadequate midwife,
wondering how in the world things ended up like this.
And it is the fullness of time.

Again, making do with what they have,
they take the feeding trough, the manger,
and use it for a basinet for the Newborn.
His coming seems so accidental,
so incidental, so random…
in the fullness of time.

This is the time chosen from the foundation of the world;
this is just what God imagined
or foresaw or even planned.
He knew the Good Shepherd
would come to his sheep as a Lamb.
While his people were harassed and helpless,
like sheep without a shepherd,
then would he come in the fullness of time.

He would take the anxious feeling of being caught short,
the time when we wonder what to do next,
this time of embarrassed helplessness,
the time of being ashamed of panic and poverty
and transfigure it—
by coming to dwell with us right here in this time—
and make it beautiful, make it his time,
the fullness of time.

Meditation on a Theme from Wesley and St. Paul

From the great halls of splendor
He stepped into the night,
To make himself our mender
In our pain and in our plight.

> He descended from the highest height
> Of joy to know our woes;
> He relinquished all his power to fight
> With weakness all our foes.

The King of kings became a slave
To know us in our need,
Quit filling all creation save
The space within a seed.

> His scepter and his staff and rod
> Were laid aside with grace,
> Yet still the glory of our God
> Shone in his human face:

His person, essence, who he is
(The Hand within the Glove)
God found in fashion as a Man,
Emptied of all but Love.

He Comes Down from Heaven

"No one has gone up to heaven
except the One who came down from heaven,
the Son of Man who is in heaven…"
John's Gospel 3:13, Jerusalem Bible

The early news wends its way…
The first preaching of the preachers say,
"The kingdom of heaven is near!
Heaven's kingdom is here!"

What is it like?
What is it like—for the One who is in heaven—
(We could almost say the One who makes heaven—heaven!)
What is it like for him to come down from heaven?
And what is more like heaven when he comes down to us?
Is heaven there or here?
Where is heaven?
With the archangels and seraphim?
Or in the womb of Mary?
And then with his birth—
The stable where ox and ass and cattle feed?
Are the angels leaving heaven
To sing their song over the hills of Bethlehem?
Or do they feel as they draw near the place of the Nativity
That they are coming to heaven—
To that Holiest Place where he who was with God in the beginning
And is God—
Is become flesh and is dwelling among us?

Think of it!
He who is at the heart of the throne in heaven,
Angels and archangels, cherubim and seraphim, powers and dominions
Worshiping and adoring him,
Hearing melodies and words that we can only dimly guess,
Songs so beautiful that our hearts would break for wonder
If we heard them,
A cataract of praise where he is able to discern
Every strand of song from every single singer—
Now plunges himself into utter silence
Until his nascent bit of embryonic humanity forms ears to hear
The flow of blood, the swish of fluid, the beating of his mother's heart.

Think of it!
He who can see everything
And dwells in the light from which heaven and earth flee away,
The light to which no one can approach—
Steps down into the darkness of our beginnings and our wanderings.
He becomes blind until he opens his eyes as a newborn
Unable to focus on a new world,
Lit by a torch or an oil lamp
Or perhaps only the light of the sinking moon
That reveals the shapes and shadows of manger and stall,
The misty breath of the cattle in the stable,
The nearness of his mother's breast
And the blurred outlines of her eyes and lips.

Think of it!
He who inhabits eternity
And for whom the nations are a drop in the bucket,
Who fills infinity enough to be everywhere,
Now confines himself to the growing seed within Mary.
He who is present in all places at all times,
Now becomes local and limited,
Centering himself down into a human baby,
Once upon a time…

Think of it!
The Word who speaks with the Father and the Holy Spirit
In the primeval counsels of eternity;
Who speaks creation into existence;
Who, in conversing with the thrones and dominions,
The angelic intelligences of the cosmos,
Imparts to them what little of his knowledge they can bear;
Who speaks and knows all that God knows—
Now relinquishes all knowledge of himself or anything else,
Knows only the trauma of being born into a strange, cold world,
No longer knows who he is,
Knows only what every human being coming into the world knows,
And like us all, with his inarticulate cries
Expresses his distress, hunger, thirst and need
Because, like us all, it is all he can say
And like us all, it is the only way he can begin to breathe
The cold night air into which he is born.

Think of it!
He who as the Only-begotten God
Wields all power and rules with all authority,
Commanding principalities and galaxies,
Governing quarks and quasars, sparrows and rainbows,
Lets go of it all and comes down from heaven,
Losing everything, becomes weak and wanting,
A baby in his mother's arms.

And yet, even though he lets heaven go
And comes down,
It seems that heaven would not be bereft of him
And so follows him to earth
And is here—
With a cloud of witnesses at his birth!

Sorrow's Son

Now Jacob halted on the road to Bethlehem
As Rachel's labor drove her life out on the limb
That ever grew more slender till at last it broke
With anguished cries and there a bitter name she spoke.

"My sorrow's son," she called the baby with her cry,
Who'd pled with Jacob, "Give me children else I die!"
Now both alternatives in answer found their mark
In dread fulfillment implacable and stark.

But Jacob loved the boy and would not let this stand.
The curse he lifted from this "son of his right hand"
And left it there near Bethlehem. Another Son
Would take this grief along with every other one

And bear them far beyond the hills of Bethlehem.
He'd take each undeservéd woe and at the rim
Of this old world somehow would bear it all and make
An end and a beginning for anyone to take.

The way to Bethlehem is more than just an end.
Travail may take us there—bring more than we can mend,
And yet out from the grief a child may come to birth.
Don't curse the new, but bless his growing here on earth!

For unto us a Child is born, who grieve along the way.
Our sins and sorrows he took up for joy at our new day.
Our Sorrow's Son, God's Benjamin, has opened wide the door
To us who scarcely stumble through to life forevermore.

A Voice in Ramah

For Rachel and for Jacob, the way to Bethlehem
Was paved with woe, for death would take but one of them
And part the lovers, who despite the parting forces,
Had loved each other from their own secret sources.

Could Rachel's barrenness have been a blessing in disguise—
The childless years postpone her travail and demise
And give her years with him who'd loved her at first sight—
Whose smitten heart was ever wounded with delight?

Those passing years had added finally a son
And now a second birth would leave her all undone—
Impart her cries unto the hills of Bethlehem,
Until she wept no longer for herself, but all of them—

Her children that are slain, a voice in Ramah heard
Still weeping for the killing that withstands the Word.

Joseph Dreams

Had the whole world gone mad?
Or was it just his little corner?
Life under the Romans was hard, but he was a good carpenter
and he could earn his living well enough.
He was not like that Joseph of old,
who had dreamed of destiny and dominion.
What he wanted, what he dreamed of was a quiet life with Mary,
loving her and providing for the children they would have together.
She had seemed like a virtuous young woman,
lovely in her love for their God, her kindness to people,
and her poetic singing of the Psalms.
Yes, he could grow old by her side
as they would help each other through the years.

But now someone had gotten in ahead of him!
His dream of having a family with Mary was crushed.
And yet she was saying that she had never known a man;
she had kept herself pure: this was the work of God's Spirit.

But what should he do?
They both were of the house and lineage of David,
descendents who kept a secret fire burning; a hope in a small corner
that some family among all their kin would be the family of Messiah.
Their women knew that a woman descended from David
would be the mother of Messiah, the Savior of their people.
Had those of David's kin looked over their shoulder and wondered
how God would bring to pass his promise within their family?
But they had never dreamed he would come this way!
They had never dreamed he would be conceived out of wedlock!
They had dreamed...but they had never dreamed of this.
Joseph had dreamed of a family,
but he had never dreamed of this trouble, sorrow, and scandal.

Who knows what he was thinking?
The people of his day had heard lots of excuses
when girls got into trouble—but never this one!
Either she was confused or misguided or she sought to misguide…
Each possibility seemed worse than the last—
Or was she telling the truth?

But in any case, what then?
If there was another man, he should get out of the way.
If she was crazy, he should get out of the way.
If she was trying to deceive, he should get out of the way.
And if it was God—for sure he should get out of the way!
All the possibilities seemed to point to one solution.
He did not want to bring any more trouble to Mary than she already had.
He would divorce her quietly.

And then he dreamed a dream…
The angel of the Lord appeared to him and said,
"Joseph, son of David, do not be afraid to take Mary home as your wife, because
what is conceived in her is of the Holy Spirit.
She will give birth to a son
and you are to give him the name of Jesus,
because he will save his people from their sins."

All that had happened to Mary accorded with God's holiness!
He need have no fear for her character, or her sanity—or his own!
God was at work and he, Joseph, was in the middle of it,
exactly where God wanted him.

It was almost as if God said to Joseph,
"You know that dream of yours,
of having a family with Mary and growing old with her?
It's not such a bad dream; in fact, I like it!
The kind of home you are dreaming of
is just what I was wanting for my Son!
I am not asking you to give up your dream of a family,
but could you make room in it for my Son?
Would you let your sons and daughters be his brothers and sisters?
Would you let your wife be his mother?
And—would you be his father here on earth?
Could you make room for Jesus?"

A Detail from "The Flight to Egypt"

The Narrow Way

"For here is great misery, proud man!
But there is greater mercy, a humble God!"
St. Augustine of Hippo

Is the narrow way by which we enter the Kingdom
Related to the narrow way by which Jesus entered our world?

How do we let this mind be in us which was also in Christ Jesus?
Paul tells us what his mind was: "Who being in the form of God,
Did not think equality with God something to be held onto,
But emptied himself… being born in human likeness…"
How do we embrace this scandal and this mystery?

Is there something about the Incarnation, the birth of Christ among us,
Which can give us grace to walk in the same humility of heart?
Is there a glory which shines from the time when God became a Child
Which can transform us into the same image from glory to glory,
So that we could enter the Kingdom as little children?

I wonder if the way Jesus entered our world
Is the same way by which we enter his world?
Perhaps our children get it right after all
When they are drawn to the Christmas Story.
Who can describe the change in our hearts
When we see the little Lord Jesus asleep on the hay?

Is there power in God's powerlessness,
In the humility of God, which can penetrate our pride,
Undo our pretensions, and open us up to his Spirit,
Which, like water, seeks the lowest place and flows there?
Be careful!—the power is in the sign, the way, the matter itself!

So heaven rejoices in God's downward mobility
And sings of peace on earth and glad tidings to all people.
"For unto you is born this day in the city of David,
A Savior, which is Christ the Lord!"
And this shall be the sign of God's humility:
"You will find a baby wrapped in swaddling clothes
And lying in a manger."

A Detail from "The Shepherds Worship the Baby"

Like Walking on Water

Immediately he made his disciples get into the boat and go before him to the other side, to Bethsaida, while he dismissed the crowd.

And after he had taken leave of them, he went up on the mountain to pray. And when evening came, the boat was out on the sea, and he was alone on the land. And he saw that they were making headway painfully, for the wind was against them. And about the fourth watch of the night he came to them, walking on the sea. He meant to pass by them, but when they saw him walking on the sea they thought it was a ghost, and cried out, for they all saw him and were terrified. But immediately he spoke to them and said, "Take heart; it is I. Do not be afraid." And he got into the boat with them, and the wind ceased. And they were utterly astounded, for they did not understand about the loaves, but their hearts were hardened.

Mark 6:45-52, ESV

Like walking on water he came to us
When the night was half spent
And the wind was against us.
When our best efforts could not move us any further…

Like walking on water he came to us,
In the impossibility of the Virgin,
In the wide eyes of her wonder,
In the humility of her trust.

Like walking on water He came to us:
In the overshadowing of the Holy Ghost,
In the brooding of the Spirit of God
Over the face of the waters of our humanity.

Like walking on water he came to us:
When from the mountainside of heaven
He saw that we were in trouble and toiling,
Toiling against sorrow and sin,
Against the chaos that would whelm over us.

Like walking on water he came to us:
On the fluid, turbulent upheaval of our condition—
Not hovering above it nor sinking beneath it,
But in contact with the troubled sea of our humanity,
Touched with the feeling of our weaknesses and infirmities.

Like walking on water he came to us:
Solid and real, not a ghost, but Incarnate,
He took hold of the gunwales of our nature with his bare hands
And hoisted himself into the same boat we are in.

Like walking on the water he came to us,
In the familiar miracle, the startling humility of his birth,
Displaying who he really is and helping us remember
From the heart what we had failed to understand.

Like walking on the water he came to us,
Born to Mary and Joseph long ago
Born our Savior, Christ the Lord,
Coming to us in the fourth watch of the night
And saying, "Take heart! It is I! Do not be afraid!"

The Water of Bethlehem

And three of the thirty chief went down, and came to David in the harvest time unto the cave of Adullam: and the troop of the Philistines pitched in the valley of Rephaim. And David was then in an hold, and the garrison of the Philistines was then in Bethlehem. And David longed, and said, "Oh that one would give me drink of the water of the well of Bethlehem, which is by the gate!" And the three mighty men brake through the host of the Philistines, and drew water out of the well of Bethlehem, that was by the gate, and took it, and brought it to David: nevertheless he would not drink thereof, but poured it out unto the LORD. And he said, "Be it far from me, O LORD, that I should do this: Is not this the blood of the men that went in jeopardy of their lives?" Therefore he would not drink of it. These things did these three mighty men.

2 Samuel 23:13-17, KJV

Prelude

The vision like a star before me
Burns with ever greater light.
By it God's Spirit does implore me
And lead me traveling through the night.
The journey's long but he is able
To lead me where he's apt to dwell:
Perhaps a cave, perhaps a stable—
I look within and find the Well.

Ballad

There is a well in Bethlehem,
The water pure and clear,
And David longed to drink from it.
Not only God and cave could hear
His wistful sigh. His men who near
To him had come from empty lives
Had three among them who took part
To please this man of God's own heart.

'Twas harvest time when they came down
To David in the hold
And overheard his heart's desire:
A simpler time, a time of old
When coming home from keeping sheep,
The well was where he would with friends,
Just by the gate their friendship keep
With drinks of water from the deep.

But now the time was not as then—
The maddened Saul did rave
And drive him from each vale and glen
Till now he hid within the cave.
The well and town which he so prized
Were held by the uncircumcised.
And he must go unrecognized,
Loved by a few, by most despised.

'Twas no command that moved the three;
They were no 'Light Brigade.'
They sought to please their uncrowned king—
Their love for him was all that made
Them carry out the daring raid.
They broke through camp and garrison
Until at last the well they won
And filled their skin for Jesse's son.

'Twas harvest time when they came back
To David in the hold
And proffered him that precious drink,
The fruit of mighty deed so bold.
They with the water there renewed
The rite of friendship as of old.
The act transcended flight and feud
And David's weary heart renewed.

He took the water skin from them
And looked up to the skies
And water poured before the Lord—
He dared not drink the sacred prize.
This was to him the blood of three
Who risked their lives in fealty.
Their friendship quenched his deeper thirst
Because they loved him from the first.

There is a well in Bethlehem,
The water deep and pure,
And thirsty souls may drink of him,
God's Son, man's only lasting cure.
Like water poured upon the ground,
He in a human frame was found;
He died for us whom sin had bound
And rose again, eternally crowned.

Of lords he has been made the Lord,
Yet still on earth we find
He is by many folks ignored,
Despised by those whose hearts are blind.
Like David, David's Son would be
Encouraged by another 'three'
Who'd strive to meet his heart's desire,
With hearts aflame from friendship's fire.

And when he in his kingdom comes
His mighty men will be
The ones whose lives were filled by his
And poured out just like David's three,
Those outcasts from society.
'Twas naught in them to be desired
But God and David them inspired.
Thus they surpassed what was required.

When David in his kingdom came,
These three were doubly blest.
For while he yet was put to shame,
They owned him king before the rest.
And we can be like them, I think,
If we to Jesus come and drink.
For nothing worthwhile in us lives
Until his life to us he gives.

There is a well in Bethlehem,
The water pure and free.
And those who've tasted say of him,
"A poured out life for all is he!"
This one has made his poured out life
For God and man the end of strife—
Yes, by him God the covenant swore
And bids us come and thirst no more.

And if we stay with him awhile
And listen to his voice,
His heart perhaps we'll overhear
And be left with the subtle choice
To merely follow his command,
Or sense his heart and with him stand.
For now's the time to own him king
And fellowship his suffering.

There is a well in Bethlehem;
From there the water flowed.
Our cup was filled with love he spilled—
Spilled at the end of Calvary's road.
The water yearns for men of might
Poured out upon his left and right,
So precious in the Father's sight—
When he shall come, his heart's delight.

And oh, did I behold a Man
More desolate than the first?
And was he hanging on a cross?
And did I hear him say, "I thirst?"
Oh, who are standing with the King,
Companions of his suffering?
'Tis harvest time again, I'm told,
and David's Son is in the hold.

A Detail from "The Young Jesus — A Carpenter"

I Will Join Myself to Them

I will join myself to them
in the blinking wandering eyes of the unknowing infant,
whose tiny little fingers curl up into little fists,
with paper thin finger nails that catch and tear
when they are caught in the threads of the blanket.

I will join myself to the faces of those
who rest by the way and sit in the sun
so bright that they must shut their eyes,
their vision filled with the blind crimson glow,
their faces warmed and weathered.

I will join myself to those who are so weary
they cannot take another step,
so burdened that their stomachs churn with dread.

I will join myself to those who dance and sing at weddings,
rejoicing with those who share out of their need
a feast for friends and loved ones.

I will join myself to the unanswerable questions,
the times of doubt and hurt,
the times of feeling alone and lost.

I will join myself forever to those who are born
and who grow and learn and live
and love and die.

I will join my nature to theirs in such a permanent way
that the union will never come undone.
Even death will only make my union with them stronger
and my rising from the dead in their flesh
that I have made my own,
will only temper the link
that I have forged with them forever.

I will join myself to them
by becoming one of them forever.
The chains of my Incarnation will be so strong
that they shall stand the strain of pulling
all my sons and daughters into life.

I will join myself to them in such a way
that Deity and Humanity
will be forever wound together within me—
inseparable in who I am as a Person.

I will join myself to them in such an intimate way
that I will save them from their sins,
their tragic waywardness,
their congenital corruption.

I will join myself to their stupid senseless choices,
their tragic failures,
their heartlessness to one another,
their greed and wickedness,
their folly for which eternity could not contain enough regret.

I will join myself to them in these things
with such a strong grip
that I will be able to pull them down with me into my death
and all will die
and all their sins I will cast down into the depths of death.

I will join myself to them,
retaining such a grip on them as persons
that I will be able to retrieve them out of death,
yet leave their sin in the grave.

I will join myself to them
and with my resurrection,
pull them into my everlasting love and life.

I will join myself to them forever;
I will join myself to them in righteousness and justice,
in love and compassion.
I will join myself to them in faithfulness,
and they will know me, the LORD.

I will join myself to them in such a way
that they will call me Jesus,
for I shall save them from their sins.

I will join myself to them
and they will call me, "Emmanuel,
God with us."

The Inscriber Within

I will put my law in their minds and write it on their hearts.
I will be their God and they shall be my people.
Jeremiah 31:35, NIV

I think of Jeremiah in a city under siege
Near the end of the world as he has known it.
The Babylonian armies are without the gates, surrounding Jerusalem.
The battering rams are swinging and pounding against the great doors
Like a dreadful drum beating out its somber sounds of doom.
The broken-hearted prophet is witnessing the breakdown
Of the covenant that God had made with his forebears.

But Jeremiah hears not only the harsh cries of the armies without,
The booming of the rams against the gates,
The conspiratorial whispers of the besieged seeking escape,
And the wailing of the dying and the bereaved—
He also hears the LORD speaking a promise,
"Behold the days are coming when I will make a new covenant
With the house of Israel and with the house of Judah.
It will not be like the covenant I made with their forefathers…
But this will be the covenant that I will make:
I will plant my Law deep within their minds and write it on their hearts…
They all shall know me… and I will forgive their iniquity…"

I think of myself, like a city under siege,
And I wonder, "O LORD, how will you do it?
How will you get inside this hard heart of mine
And remain long enough to write your Law on the tablets of my heart?
Will you batter the door down
With the battering rams of your great power and might?
And if you came in that way, how would you proceed?
Like the ravaging Chaldeans of old? Is there any other way?

"Deep within them will I plant my Law…"
How will you do it?
Could you change me so radically that I would want to follow you
And walk in your ways—that doing your will would come naturally?
Your righteousness would spring from the deepest part of me
And would be the expression of what I am at the core?
How could you accomplish such a renovation of personality
Without obliterating who I am?

"Not by might, nor by power, but by my Spirit!" declares the LORD.
"My Spirit will overshadow a virgin,
One who, because she has not known a man, cannot bear a child,
And I will cause her to conceive and bear a Son
and she shall call his name,
Immanuel, 'God with us.'"

"Instead of breaking down the walls and battlements of humanity,
I will come among them as an infant, a child who is one of them.
I will bind my nature to theirs
and I will know them
and they shall all know me
From the least of them to the greatest of them,
For I will take their rebellion upon myself;
I will bear their sins and sorrows
And though they slay me, they shall not prevail,
For in slaying me, I shall slay their sin and iniquity
And I shall bear their sorrows into the grave,
And I will forgive their iniquity and remember their sin no more."

"I will turn their enmity into friendship,
And just as the most hardened human being
Drops his defenses at the sight of a small baby,
So I will get past their defenses incognito,
As an infant, binding my future to theirs.
And there within their hearts I will establish my throne,
And they will know that I am the LORD."

"Instead of the battering rams of might and power,
I will use the key of my humility and love,
And open the door to their hearts:
I will use the key of who I am.
And I who created them in my image in the first place,
Will touch the tumblers in the lock
Seemingly rusted in place for having never been used
Because no key had ever fit the lock as yet,
But I who created them, know them despite their fallen condition,
And I know the combinations to the hidden door,
For I am the Key that fits the lock."

"And I will help them find the inner room,
That door at the back of their hearts,
The hidden source and the secret spring,
The inner mountain for the giving of the Law,
The hidden Zion that I have loved,
And I will inscribe who I am, my nature and my name,
My grace and my love, my justice and my holiness,
My mercy and my truth—
On that inner untouched and unreached surface,
Because only I can truly reach it."

"And there I will plant my Law,
And I will make each heart a city of peace ruled by her Redeemer,
In love with him who first loved her and gave himself for her,
In his coming in her flesh,
And in his dying of her death,
And in his rising from the dead,
Like the first birth at the dawn of a new world."

A Detail from "The Shepherds Worship the Baby"

Psalms and Songs

A Detail from "Moses Leads Israel through the Red Sea"

The Waters Saw You

The waters saw you, O God,
the waters saw you and writhed;
the very depths were convulsed.
The clouds poured down water,
the skies resounded with thunder;
your arrows flashed back and forth.
Your thunder was heard in the whirlwind,
your lightning lit up the world;
the earth trembled and quaked.
Your path led through the sea,
your way through the mighty waters,
though your footprints were not seen.

You led your people like a flock
by the hand of Moses and Aaron.
Psalm 77:16-20, NIV

The waters saw you, O God!
The waters above the heavens stood back in amazement.
The thrones and dominions were made to listen with humble shepherds,
as the hosts of heaven became a choir singing,
"Glory to God in the highest,
and on earth, peace, good will among all people!"

The gates of hell trembled;
all Jerusalem wondered;
the counsels of the tyrant were troubled
when the first worshippers from the nations,

came as Wise Men from the East,
came as an offering of first fruits,
a harbinger of the glory of all the nations
that shall come and bow before you.

Your way led down from the highest heavens,
your path through the mighty heavens…
The waters trembled and stirred
as the Spirit of God moved on the face of the deep
in the overshadowing of the Holy Ghost
and you were carried in the womb of the Virgin.

The waters trembled and broke as you came into this world;
they stood back, as you were born in Bethlehem.
The earth shuddered and quaked at the footfalls of shepherds
who searched and found the stable in the frosty night
and saw you wrapped in swaddling clothes, lying in a manger.

The waters saw you, O God!
They trembled in amazement at your humility
when you came to be baptized by John in the River Jordan.
John stood back and at first refused to plunge you into the stream,
but you insisted and as the waters receded from you,
the heavens parted in wonder, and some thought they heard thunder,
but the Father spoke,
"This is my beloved Son in whom I am well pleased!"

The waters saw you, O God,
the waters at the bottom of Jacob's well in Samaria.
They stood back to make way for a greater and older Stream—
For you offered Living Water to the woman at the well
and she went and told the people of Sychar who flowed
like a stream out of the town
to hear your words of hope and fulfillment.

The waters saw you, O God,
the waters in the eyes of those who had no hope,
who thought they could never come to you.
They heard the good news of forgiveness
and the heavens trembled and the earth shook
when you began to make a way for your people.
The storm broke and the waters flowed in the tears
of the woman who had been used by others all her life.
She trembled and quaked
as sobs of gratitude and relief wracked her frame
and she knelt and washed your feet with the streams
that sprang from her healing heart and flowed from her eyes.
And she who was forgiven much, loved you all the more.

The waters saw you, O God,
the waters saw you and writhed:
the very depths were convulsed.
The clouds poured down water,
the skies resounded with thunder;
your arrows flashed back and forth.
Your thunder was heard in the whirlwind,
your lightning lit up the world:
the Sea of Galilee trembled and quaked.
The disciples cried out in fear and desperation,
"Master, don't you care that we are drowning?"
Then you awoke and stood up and rebuked the wind
and said to the waves, "Peace! Be still!"
The lake became a sea of glass, so still and calm.
The disciples exchanged one fear for another:
in holy awe they asked each other, "Who is this?
Even the winds and the waves obey him!"

On another time when you sent your disciples
to the other side of the Sea of Galilee,
you saw that the wind was contrary against them
and you beheld them straining at the oars.
They could not make it on their own
and were foundering in the midst of the sea.
Your path led through the sea,
your way through the mighty waters
though your footprints were not seen.
You walked on the water to rescue the men you loved
and when they cried out in fear and terror,
you comforted them and said, "Do not be afraid, it is I!"
And they found themselves on the other side.

The waters of the adversary saw you and trembled.
The demons and the powers
relinquished their hold on the oppressed;
the monsters of the sea coughed up their prey;
even the Leviathan of death lost its grip
as you, the Good Shepherd,
began to call your loved ones by name.

The soldiers, too, who came with Judas to take you,
fell to the ground—
and all you said was, "I am!"
The earth trembled and quaked, and the rocks rent
as you gave your life upon the tree.
There the waters of sin and death stood back,
the sun withdrew its shining,
and darkness came over all the land
from the sixth hour to the ninth.
And the oceans within God parted,
as God stood back from God
and you cried out from the rending and the tearing
"Why have you forsaken me?"

You made a way for us into the holiest.
In your own brokenness of body and heart,
you saved us from ourselves,
and rescued us from a Tyrant more terrible than Pharaoh.
You loved us and gave yourself for us.
And the earth stood back and the heavens stood back,
and you made a way where there was no way,
descending where none had ever gone,
ascending where none could ever go,
filling the whole universe with your salvation,
rising from death and leading us all in your train.

Your path led through the sea,
your way through the mighty waters
though your footprints were not seen.

You led your people like a flock,
by your own hand as our Good Shepherd—
our Lord Jesus.

A Giving of Thanks

Thank you Lord Jesus for creating us.
You spoke of us with your Father before the worlds.
You thought of the beginning, the morning of creation,
The freshness, the wonder, the possibilities and the price
Of what it would cost to bring creation
To its end, its consummation,
Its eternal reconciliation
With the Father and the Son and the Holy Ghost.
And for all that, you decided it was worth
The plunging of your hands into the earth.

Like a Song

Like a song, Jesus came to live among us
And took up our laments and praises.
He sang them himself, not only with his voice,
But with all his heart and soul, all his mind and strength.
He sang to the Father and to us with perfect pitch,
In the unmistakable timbre of his life—
As only he could do, as only he would do.

Before he came, the prophets had heard snatches of the music,
Strains on the air which had filled them with longing and delight.
They had tried to set words to the music
But the music itself was as elusive as it was beautiful,
And all they succeeded in doing was to increase the longing.

And then beyond hope, beyond our most imaginative dreams
He came to live among us—like a song!
At last, the words and the music came together in him.
Very God of very God—and very human, too!
At last, full Deity and full humanity came together in him.
The Word became flesh and dwelt among us,
And we heard the song of the humanity of God.

We heard at last, in the strains of the lost chord
The song of the Only-begotten of the Father,
Full of grace and truth, beginning to be sung
With heaven rejoicing, and shepherds praising…
And the music of the Glory in the little Lord Jesus
With his crying, his cooing, and his sighing,
Showing how God had joined his condition to ours
Becoming our song in the night.

Like a song he came to live among us,
"Of the Father's love begotten ere the worlds began to be,"
Our Lord Jesus, born in Bethlehem, who—
"For us and for our salvation came down from heaven,"
Singing the love that will not let us go.

A Detail from "The Angels Proclaim to the Shepherds the Good News about the Birth of the Savior"

A Psalm for the Incarnation

We praise and thank you,
Infinite, immortal, immutable God—

That when you limited yourself to our humanity
For our sakes,
We beheld the humanity of your infinite love.

When you tasted death for us all—
We who sat in that darkness—
We saw the great light of your life.

When you underwent the changes of our condition—
You learned, grew, got tired, hungered, thirsted—
Somehow we discerned your changeless identity,
We saw that you are Jesus Christ,
The same yesterday, today and forever.

We praise and thank you
That when you dwelt among us,
You revealed to us
What you have been like all along.

We praise and thank you
That when you dwelt among us,
We beheld your glory,
The glory as of the Only-begotten of the Father,
Full of grace and truth.
Amen.

Canticle of the Stairs

O my dove
That art in the clefts of the rock,
In the secret places of the stairs,
Let me see thy countenance,
Let me hear thy voice,
For sweet is thy voice,
And thy countenance is comely.
Song of Solomon 2:14, KJV

Like a dove alighting and resting in the cleft of the rock,
So you, Lord God, by your Spirit overshadowed Mary
Who became the cleft of the rock in our human condition
Hidden beneath the shadow of your wings where you came

Down in the secret places of the stairs.
Did you come down the tiny spiral staircase,
The genetic ladder that contains the blueprint
In the secret place, in the cleft of the rock?

In the secret of the cell, the cleft of the rock…
As the little spiral stair unwinds to form a gamete
In order to unite with another to form a new ladder of life,
A plan for a person, a riverbed for personality—

Did your incomplete ladder join with the Virgin's
To form a new secret stair by which you
Could descend into our humanity and become flesh?
In the clefts of the rock, in the secret of the stairs?

If only we could see your face…
If only we could hear your voice…
Your face and your voice were written on the ladder,
On the tiny stairs stretching from heaven to earth,

Conceived by the Holy Ghost in the secret places of the stairs,
Born of the Virgin Mary in the cleft of the rock,
In the cave become stable housing beasts, perhaps doves,
We first saw your face and first heard your voice

In the little Lord Jesus nesting in the hay, lying in a manger,
Our Little Dove wrapped in swaddling clothes.
Your voice is sweet and we hear it in the cooing
And crying of this little one in the cleft of Mary's arms.

Your countenance is comely and comforting,
Lovely beyond our wildest hopes because you came down,
Becoming one of us, revealing the beauty
Of your meekness, the comeliness of your love.

O my dove
That art in the clefts of the rock,
In the secret places of the stairs,
Let me see thy countenance,
Let me hear thy voice;
For sweet is thy voice
And thy countenance is comely.

Cousin Elizabeth

From Elizabeth's greeting to Mary and her response
Luke 1:39-56

I had a Cousin Elizabeth,
A delightful old lady
Who lived in an old tree-lined neighborhood
In New Brunswick, New Jersey.
I had no claim on her other than
She was my grandmother's first cousin.
We called our grandmother, Meme.

Cousin Elizabeth was a daughter of Meme's father's sister, whom Meme called Aunt Jenny. She was a woman with spunk. Aunt Jenny left the South under Reconstruction and despite resistance from some of her family, went to nursing school in Philadelphia where she was taught by a pupil of Florence Nightingale.

As you might have guessed, Aunt Jenny was a suffragette, practiced nursing, and married a doctor. She passed on her love of family, her love of nursing, and her gumption to her daughter Elizabeth, who kept up with her cousins in the South during the hard times of the twenties and thirties. Cousin Elizabeth was Meme's favorite cousin. Meme would glow whenever she came. I have a photo of the northern cousins and the southern cousins sitting together on a settee and Meme is beaming.

We each of us need a Cousin Elizabeth
Who believes the best of us,
Who honors and cheers us on,
Who recognizes the miracle within us,
Who carries a witness within who
Leaps for joy when we arrive.

We each of us need a Cousin Elizabeth,
Who has tasted disappointment and sorrow,
Who understands life when it does not conform to the ideal,
Who, because she has received a great Mercy,
Knows how to be merciful to us.

We each of us need a Cousin Elizabeth,
Who bears within herself the work of the free Spirit of God,
Who knows what we know without explanation or justification,
Who can call forth from us—a Magnificat.

Tom Worth's grandmother, Meme, with her sisters and cousins. Meme is on the right; she is looking at her cousin Elizabeth sitting next to her.
From a photograph circa 1959.

From Wrath to Beauty

A Christmas Meditation from Psalm 90, A Prayer of Moses, the Man of God

LORD, you have been our dwelling place
through every generation that has existed on this globe.
And what were you like before creation?
Before the mountains were heaved up into the sky
or this planet was formed,
you were who you were and are.
From everlasting to everlasting you have existed
in the beauty of your holiness and love,
in the glory of all that you were before the world was,
all that you will be, beyond the unfolding renewal of the world.

We, by contrast, have for so long been under this regime of finitude,
of the silent working of endings,
forever withering what was blooming,
bringing death to the living, loss to the loving…
And those who learned the ropes of this regime of wrath
taught us how to number our days
and live wisely while we yet lived.

But we ask you, O God, like Moses your friend has asked you—
to relent, to turn, to repent.
There must be something more than the prudent expenditure
of the time that we have.
The fact that we return to dust
is in itself a reminder of the original prediction.
Life passes so quickly and evanescently that, dreamlike,
we dissolve into the primary elements at the end.
The forward push of time
plows like a ship through the ocean of our existence.
And what is left in its wake,

but the closing waves of the sea of things as they were and always are?
Not only our lifetimes, but the centuries and the millennia
pass like the watches of the night itself.
We come and go...
And is this all there is?
Satisfy us, nourish us,
sustain us with that which is truly substantial—
even consubstantial with the Father and the Holy Ghost:
Your unfailing love, your covenant loyalty,
your merciful faithfulness, your faithful mercy—
so we may sing and have joy amid the relentless return to dust.

May the beauty of the LORD rest upon us...
the beauty which was with the Father and the Holy Spirit,
that glory, beauty, favor,
that incalculable grace which brings death to death,
subverts the regime of wrath, abrogates it
and supplants it with the nature and character of Jesus:
the glory of his centrally eccentric love for us—
his love for us dust-bound glimpses of human hope and yearning—
longing for something permanent,
something beyond the dust, something after it and before it—
that which is from everlasting to everlasting.

Let the beauty of the LORD, let his favor rest upon us—
yes!—that beauty that dwells at the Father's side,
the glory of the Only-Begotten
who came when shepherds were abiding in the fields,
keeping watch over their flocks by night.
And did this watch in the night seem like a thousand years
or the day which had just gone by?
And did we hear the heavenly hosts singing,
Glory to God in the highest,
and on earth (where wrath had reigned) peace,
to us on whom his favor (oh so unmerited!) now rested?
Let the beauty of the LORD rest upon us!

Bring a torch, Jeanette, Isabella! Bring a torch, to the cradle run!
It is Jesus, good folk of the village, Christ is born and Mary's calling,
Ah! Ah! Beautiful is the Mother! Ah! Ah! Beautiful is her Son.

Arise, shine, for your Light has come;
and the Glory, the Beauty of the LORD, has risen upon you!

"The Woman Clothed with the Sun."
(Detail from a Painting, "The Church of Jesus Christ.")

Parallel and Paradox

"The Flight to Egypt"

Resolution

It has been said that the strongest force in music
Is the drive for the tonic.
No matter where the melody and harmonies go,
they will seek resolution in the key
in which the piece is written.
If we hear a piece in the key of C, we are never satisfied
until the melody finally ends and culminates in the C note.

We long for resolution,
not only in music but in almost everything in life.
Sometimes, the only thing that keeps us going
is knowing we have not gotten to the end of the story.
The whole creation groans, waiting for resolution.

Some would say the best preparation for the Second Coming
is to understand the End Time prophecies correctly.
But I maintain that the best preparation
for the Second Coming of Christ
is to apprehend his First Coming.
"Because the beginning shall remind us of the end."

When the whole world will own the Prince of Peace, their King.
Heaven and nature will sing,
"Glory to God in the highest heaven
and on earth, peace, goodwill among people!"

This music of the gospel,
"the glad tidings which shall be for all people,"
was written in the key of the Incarnation.
And when all is said and done,
it must resolve itself in that keynote
in profound and eternal ways.

A Sign

*"And this shall be a sign to you, you will find a baby
wrapped in swaddling clothes and lying in a manger."*
Luke 2:12

Who knew?
Well, the shepherds knew.
After all, the angel told them what the sign was.
They would find their Messiah
as a newborn baby lying in a manger—
That was the sign.

But in its way, the sign signified that none knew.
"The ox knows his master,
the donkey his owner's manger,
but Israel does not know,
my people do not understand."
So the ox and the donkey knew where they belonged,
And they were there in the stable.
And the donkey knew where to find nourishment—in his manger.
But now the Lord of the world comes to his people
And they do not know,
his people do not understand.

Who knows?
Well, Bethlehem does not know,
bursting at the seams because of the hassle of this census.
Augustus, who ordains the census because he desires to know,
does not know,
neither does the governor of the province.
The empire does not know.
The known world does not know.

But Mary knows.
This exhausted young mother,
doubly weary from the labor of childbirth and a long journey—
she knows if anyone does—
she knows.
She who fashions the sign, the tableau:
A baby wrapped in swaddling clothes and lying in a manger—
If anyone knows, she knows
and yet she ponders this thing in her heart.

And he who helped to fashion the sign,
Joseph, who took the insignificant manger and used it
for a purpose unknown and unforeseen by its owner—
(even the donkey knows his owner's manger)
who copes with the evolving situation
by dreaming dreams and listening to angels—
What does he know?
He knows that, as upright as he had tried to be,
he had still misjudged his beloved.
He had not known; he had not understood.
But he also knows that he shall call his foster son, Jesus,
And that he shall save his people
(who do know, who do not understand)
from their sins.
Righteous as he is, he has begun to know
that he needs to be saved and that somehow
this baby lying in a manger will do it—
is doing it already!

We read the account and we know that Luke,
who is telling this story that happened in those days
when the decree went out from Caesar Augustus—
we know that Luke knows.
But do you know?
Do I?
Are you and I included in those few,
those happy few, who know and are glad they know?
Are we somehow participants in what so many did not know,
Because we are believing back into the story?

Who knows?
Well, there's Mary and Joseph,
And the shepherds, surprised out of their wits—they know.
And you and I, we know.
Oh, yes!—
And *all* of Heaven.

A Christmas Memory

On a cold winter's night that was so deep,
Mom and Dad bundled us into the white 1959 Chevrolet
with those enormous fins that were like eyebrows
over ancient red Egyptian eyes.
I was in third grade.

We went to a Christmas open house
at West Keansburg Elementary the night before the holidays.
I can see all of us crowded into my third grade classroom—
parents, my classmates, our siblings.

My teacher, Mrs. Lucas, was wearing a blue knit dress.
Smiling, she invited us to sing some Christmas carols.
Our family was standing in the back, not far from one of the doors.

I remember as we sang "The First Noël,"
hearing Dad's clear true baritone beside me.
As we neared the end of the refrain, he reached for, found and held
those high notes on the fourth Noël.

Something began to sink in about Christmas—
this was important; this was significant.
It was worth Dad going to all that trouble
to sing so that he could be heard,
among all these grown-ups with their children
in suburban middle-class America during the last few days of 1960,
singing, or half-singing the old familiar carol.

It's funny how a held note,
and Dad glancing down at me
with a twinkle in his eye as he sang and held it,
can hang in the mind like a star—
take its rest
in the northwest,
both stop and stay,
right over the place where Jesus lay.

A Detail from "The Angels Proclaim to the Shepherds the Good News about the Birth of the Savior"

Like Water to Wine

From Jesus' beginning of miracles at the marriage at Cana in Galilee
John 2:1-11.

When we had fallen short, when we had run out,
When there was no more—then!
Like water to wine, he came to live among us,
Supplying our lack, making up the difference
In such a way that many never noticed.
But some remarked that they had never before
Tasted wine like this.

The servants in the back room knew,
They who had drawn the virgin water,
They knew, and his Mother knew.
She had pointed out the need in the first place,
She, who had known her own lack but who had said,
"Let it be to me according to your word,"
Was now telling the servants,
"Whatever he tells you, do it!"

Like water to wine he came to live among us
Bringing the vintage of eternity into our mortality,
Bringing the new wine of a great gladness:
For he who loves people loves their joy,
And especially the joy of those who in the direst need,
Made a wedding out of their own lack, welcoming more guests
Who would make their meagre provision run out even sooner.
So he would bless them with his Presence,
And turn their water to wine.

And not just any wine but the finest of wines,
The best wine, saved for last, saved for the end,
Who would destroy the shroud that enfolds all peoples,
Who would swallow up death forever,
And save the best wine for last,
Wiping the tears from all faces,
Because he who loves people loves their joy,
Bringing in the wine of a great new gladness—
Of glad tidings of great joy for all people,
"For unto you is born in the city of David a Savior…"

For the end shall be like the beginning,
That beginning of miracles where his disciples
Saw His glory and believed in him.

And now, like water to wine,
The Word was made flesh and dwelt among us,
Mingling what he is with what we are,
Taking the water of our humanity
And transforming it into the wine of a new kind of humanity,
Born of the Virgin Mary, born in Bethlehem
And offering to us, everything that we had run short of—
Joy and love, peace on earth, and goodwill to all.

Light in Darkness

The Light shines in the darkness and the darkness has not overcome it.
John 1:5 RSV

The Light which shines in the darkness is a kenotic kind of light.
He empties himself of all his power and brilliance
    which would have consumed us in a flash.

He is truly the Light which the darkness cannot overshadow or comprehend.
The darkness would have understood a power play,
    a flash of unimaginable brightness: power overpowering power.
And the darkness, holding all humanity hostage, as it were,
    would have triumphed in its own obliteration,
    because we would have perished, too.

Instead this Light shines by his grace and his truth,
    his beauty and his faithfulness,
    his holiness and his love, his care and his compassion,
    his pathos and humor in dealing with the human enigma.

Like a candle shining in a mine
    to show us the way out, so he came,
    not as the sun to banish all shadows
    and turn all to brilliant white,
    but to show us the way, step by step,
    out of our prisons, out of our darkness.

He is so small and subtle!
He is so insignificant in his coming that no one notices
     the homeless couple making do with a cave or a stable,
     their lodging for the night,
     a place for Mary to give birth to her firstborn Son.
This Light, emptied of all his brilliance, crying in the night,
     coming to live among us—and, as if he could not help himself—
     shines nonetheless—shines in our hearts—
     to give the Light of the knowledge of the glory of God
     in the very human face of the little Lord Jesus,
     nestled in his Mother's arms, asleep on the hay.

A Detail from "Peter Walks on Water"

Little Hands, Little Feet

Little hands,
Little feet,
Clutching at the air,
Kicking…
Crying as little lungs
Take in air for the first time.
Eyes wandering aimlessly,
Unable to focus.
Blinking.
Yawning.
Stretching.
Nursing.
Messing.
Sleeping.
Totally helpless.
God became like that once,
To help us.
Immanuel,
God with us:
Jesus.

"The Birth of Christ"

World Challenge

World Challenge and our poet Thomas Ryder Worth have had a positive and meaningful impact upon my life, as they have with countless others. We are all different. Like different colors and textures of thread, God has woven our varied and differing paths together to bring glory to Himself and through this amazing collection of poems shine the beauty of his Son. Like many, I became familiar with the World Challenge legacy when I read *The Cross and the Switchblade* and as a boy saw the movie. I was captivated by the story and the characters, but more importantly, nothing to that point in my life had shown me the wonder and sheer power of Jesus to bring hope, and to rescue people from the lowest estate, as that story still does.

As an adult, I came across a copy of the book at a flea market along with *The Lost Coin,* the story of the first Christian coffeehouse in New York—a World Challenge ministry. I re-read them and almost immediately moved to New York to begin helping people with life-controlling problems. There I met Gary Wilkerson, the current president of World Challenge. We became friends and I was privileged to minister alongside him and be there for the founding of the amazing Times Square Church.

During those same years, our author Thomas Ryder Worth and I had opportunity to minister together with World Challenge in New York and even visit Bulgaria as some of the first western missionaries to go to that country after the fall of communism. The most meaningful thing he did, however, was to reveal Jesus from the Scriptures in a way that was tangibly real and sincerely personal. His exposition was the powerful prose and poetry that was the "other side of the coin" to the miraculous real-life impact we were experiencing every day through the ministry of World Challenge in New York and around the world.

After many years, God has brought us back together, weaving our lives and experiences into a richly varied fabric that we hope shows you Jesus. One that helps you know him better and more personally in a way that will truly enrich your life. We hope you are enlivened by this beautiful book and the ones that will follow it in the months and years to come.

As mentioned in the acknowledgement, this exquisite collection would not be possible without the sponsorship of World Challenge. I hope you will get to know the ministry, or get re-acquainted with them. Today, Gary has personally carried the light to seventy nations, and World Challenge is active in over a dozen countries, doing amazing work, from empowering, encouraging, and equipping you in your daily faith through their teaching, sermons, devotions, books and music; to the International Pastors' Conferences and Evangelistic Crusades, to its World Poverty Solutions ministry bringing an end to poverty in some of the poorest places in the world. Please support them in the important work to which God has called them— building on the legacy, loving in the present, and looking to the future. You can learn more on the website, by calling, or on social media.

WORLD CHALLENGE | 1125 Kelly Johnson Blvd, Suite 321 | Colorado Springs, CO 80920
www.WorldChallenge.org | (719) 487-7888